Get pupils' knowledge in order with CGP!

Looking for a simple way to help pupils learn all the key facts and methods for Year 6 English? Well, look no further — this Knowledge Organiser is the perfect solution!

We've condensed each topic down to the essentials, so it covers exactly what pupils need, with clear examples and tables.

And that's not all! There's a matching Year 6 English Knowledge Retriever — a great way of making sure pupils have got to grips with the content of every page.

CGP – still the best! ☺

Our sole aim here at CGP is to produce the highest quality books — carefully written, immaculately presented and dangerously close to being funny.

Then we work our socks off to get them out to you — at the cheapest possible prices.

Published by CGP.

Editors: Siân Butler, Robbie Driscoll, Nathan Mair, Georgina Paxman

With thanks to Emma Crighton and Juliette Green for the proofreading.

With thanks to Alice Dent for the copyright research.

ISBN: 978 1 78908 962 2

Printed by Elanders Ltd, Newcastle upon Tyne.
Clipart from Corel®

Based on the classic CGP style created by Richard Parsons.

Contents

Grammar Basics

Nouns

Nouns: words that name things

① **Concrete nouns**: things you can see, touch, smell or hear

> banana   mountain

② **Abstract nouns**: names for ideas, concepts or feelings

> happiness   childhood

③ **Collective nouns**: names for groups of people or things

> a flock of sheep

Determiners

Determiners tell you if a noun is specific:

> this apple   those people

Or if it's general:

> some elves   a scarf

> five cans

They can tell you who or what owns something or how many of something there are.

> her giraffe

Verbs

Verbs: doing or being words

The frog jumped.   I am hungry.

A **modal verb** is a verb that shows how possible or certain something is.

I might start a jigsaw.   I must go to the dentist.

Adjectives & Adverbs

Adjectives describe nouns.

EXAMPLE

adjectives
the vibrant blanket was colourful
noun

Pronouns

Pronouns replace nouns.

Amy gasped when she saw herself.

The pronouns 'she' and 'herself' replace the word 'Amy'.

Phrases

Phrase: a group of words that either doesn't have a verb, doesn't have a subject or has neither

Prepositions tell you where things are in relation to each other. They can also tell you when or why things happen.

A **preposition phrase** starts with a preposition.

under the table

A **noun phrase** contains a noun and any words that describe it.

the ageing dog with floppy ears

Adverbs can describe:

1. verbs → I ate quickly.
2. adjectives → He is really happy.
3. other adverbs → We ran very fast.

Adverbs can also show possibility.
↳ Perhaps I will go.

Clauses

Main clause: usually has a subject and a verb, and makes sense on its own

Subordinate clause: gives extra information, but doesn't make sense on its own

EXAMPLE

Alex whistled while listening to music.

main clause   subordinate clause

Relative clause: a subordinate clause that gives extra information about a noun

EXAMPLE

I found a shell which was spiky.

relative pronoun   relative clause

Possessive pronouns tell you who something belongs to.

their book   our house

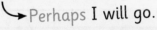

Relative pronouns introduce relative clauses.

It was Tim who heard the noise.

Sentences & Tenses

Conjunctions

Conjunctions: words or phrases that join two sentences or parts of a sentence to help your writing flow

Co-ordinating conjunctions join two main clauses.

It was cold, but we stayed at the beach until it got dark.

Subordinating conjunctions introduce a subordinate clause.

Linking Paragraphs

Paragraphs can be linked:

1 with adverbial phrases.

EXAMPLE

It often rains in Wales.
Despite this, many people go there on holiday.

An adverbial phrase is a group of words that acts like an adverb.

2 by repeating a word or phrase.

EXAMPLE

...so we usually pack a picnic when we go to the park. Often, we take my grandma with us.
My grandma is a very funny person. She always...

Active & Passive

Active voice: The subject does something to the object.

Rose spilt the beans.

Passive voice: Something is done to the subject.

The beans were spilt by Rose.

'by' can introduce the person doing the action.

Subject & Object

Subject: the person or thing doing the verb

These rules are only true for active sentences.

Seth ate a pineapple.

Object: the person or thing that has the verb done to it

Present Tense & Past Tense

Tense	Describes something that	Example
Simple present	happens regularly or is still happening	I play the trumpet.
Simple past	has already happened	I played the trumpet.

Present & Past Progressive

Present progressive: shows that something is still happening

are / am / is ✚ verb ✚ ing

Ahmet is reading.

Past progressive: shows that something was happening

were / was ✚ verb ✚ ing

Freya was painting a picture.

The Perfect Form

Present perfect: shows that something has already happened

have / has ✚ main verb

Gideon has lived on six planets.

Past perfect: shows that something happened before now, and before something else happened

had ✚ main verb

Charlie had bought balloons before the party started.

Ellipsis

Ellipsis: when an expected word or phrase is removed from a sentence

EXAMPLE

Sam is ready for school, but Kesia isn't.

'ready for school' is missing

Ellipsis helps your sentences to flow by avoiding unnecessary repetition.

Punctuation Basics

Capital Letters

Always use capital letters:

1. at the start of sentences.
2. for proper nouns.
3. for the word 'I'.

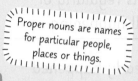

Proper nouns are names for particular people, places or things.

EXAMPLE

On Wednesday, I am going to London with John.

Ending a Sentence

.	at the end of most sentences, especially statements
?	at the end of a question
	with exclamations and some commands
!	when something is said loudly or shows strong emotion

Commas

To separate items in a list

I bought bread, cheese, carrots and a kangaroo burger from the supermarket.

Uses of Commas

'Fronted' means 'at the start of a sentence'.

After fronted adverbials

On Sunday, we ate croissants for breakfast.

To add extra information

See page 7.

To avoid ambiguity

She likes painting dogs and chess.

= She likes painting pictures of dogs.

She likes painting, dogs and chess.

= She likes both painting and dogs.

After subordinate clauses

If you see a lion, don't give it a belly rub.

Only use a comma if the subordinate clause comes before the main clause.

Adding Extra Information

Add extra information to a sentence using pairs of:

Brackets: George (who lives in a castle) likes fighting dragons.

Commas: George, who lives in a castle, likes fighting dragons.

Dashes: George — who lives in a castle — likes fighting dragons.

The extra information is called a parenthesis.

Stephanie walked home.

Where are you going?

What a nice day!

I can't believe it!

Paragraphs

Use a new paragraph for a new subject, place, time or speaker.

> Remember to leave a space or a blank line before starting each new paragraph.

> "Ahoy there! Can you see any ships?" Captain Forkbeard asked the lookout at the top of the ship's mast.
>
> New speaker ⟶ "There's one to the south," came the reply, "and it looks like it's carrying enough gold to buy us a new parrot each!"
>
> New time ⟶ Ten minutes later, the pirates were ready to attack: the cannons were loaded, the boarding ladders were set up and the crew had sharpened their cutlasses.
>
> New place ⟶ The other ship, however, was no ordinary treasure ship. Hidden below deck lay not gold bars, but soldiers, sent to arrest the pirates and restore peace to the sea.

More Punctuation

Colons

Colons can be used to introduce a list.

EXAMPLE

We're missing four ingredients that we need for our cake: flour, eggs, sugar and butter.

The part before the colon must be a main clause.

Colons can join two main clauses where one explains the other.

EXAMPLE

I can't go to school today: I'm not very well.

Semi-colons

Semi-colons can join two related main clauses.

The mouse in my house loves cheese; I always leave some out for him.

You can also use them to separate long items in a list.

This often happens when the items include other punctuation marks, such as commas.

At the pool, we saw an old, friendly lady; an angry-looking man (who I'd seen earlier); and lots of excited children.

Dashes & Hyphens

You can use a dash to separate two main clauses.

EXAMPLE

I saw Sophia yesterday evening — she was at the new cinema.

 its & it's

its = belonging to it

it's = 'it is' or 'it has'

whose & who's

whose = belonging to whom

who's = 'who is' or 'who has'

Unlike with commas, you need a semi-colon before the last item.

Hyphens join words together:

> **EXAMPLE**
> mother-in-law

They also make it clear which word an adjective describes.

> **EXAMPLE**
> a light-blue suitcase

'light' describes the shade of blue, not the weight of the suitcase.

Apostrophes

Apostrophes have two main uses:

1 to show where letters are missing

do not	don't
I am	I'm
would have	would've
will not	won't

2 to show who or what owns something

the platypus belonging to James	=	James's platypus
the yak belonging to the teachers	=	the teachers' yak
the leopard belonging to Evie	=	Evie's leopard
the goat belonging to the children	=	the children's goat

Punctuating Speech

Inverted commas can also be called speech marks.

New line when someone speaks.

comma

Final punctuation goes inside the speech marks.

Khalid asked, "Will we see sharks?"

"If we go now," replied the diver, "we'll see lots!"

inverted commas

Don't use a capital letter if the sentence carries on from before.

Prefixes, Suffixes & Word Endings

Key Words

Prefix: a group of letters at the start of a word

Suffix: a group of letters that is added to the end of a word

Root word: the word a prefix or suffix is added to

Hyphenating Prefixes

Use a hyphen to add a prefix:

1 ...if the prefix ends in a vowel and the root word starts with a vowel.

EXAMPLE

re + explain = re-explain

2 ...to avoid similar words being confused.

EXAMPLE

recovered vs. re-covered

I recovered from my illness.

I re-covered the dish.

Prefixes

Prefix	Meaning	Example
'semi'	half, partly	semicircle
'bi'	two	bicycle
'tele'	distance	television
'tri'	three	triangle
'trans'	across, through	transform
'photo'	light	photograph
'aero'	air	aeroplane
'micro'	small	microscope
'circum'	around	circumnavigate

The spelling of the root word never changes when you add a prefix.

Words ending in 'fer'

When you add a suffix to a word ending in 'fer', sometimes you double the 'r' and sometimes you don't.

Suffixes & Word Endings

Sometimes, words end with similar sounds but are spelt differently.

Sounds like...	Spellings	Examples
'shus'	cious, tious, xious	spacious, cautious, anxious
'shul'	cial, tial	facial, partial
'unt'	ent, ant	present, assistant
'unce'	ance, ence	balance, silence
'uncy'	ancy, ency	vacancy, currency
'ubul'	able, ible	dependable, possible
'ubly'	ibly, ably	visibly, reliably

Word Ending Rules

'shus' → If the root word ends in 'ce', use the spelling 'cious'.

'shul' → 'cial' is common after a vowel, and 'tial' is common after a consonant.

'ubul' & 'ubly' → Use 'able' or 'ably' when you can hear a complete root word and 'ible' or 'ibly' when you can't.

Tip: Say the new word out loud. If the 'fer' is stressed (emphasised), double the 'r'. If it's not, then don't.

EXAMPLE

refer + ing = referring

refer + ence = reference

refer + ed = referred

Confusing Words

'ei' & 'ie' Words

Learn the rule: <u>'i' before 'e' except after 'c' if the vowel sound rhymes with bee.</u>

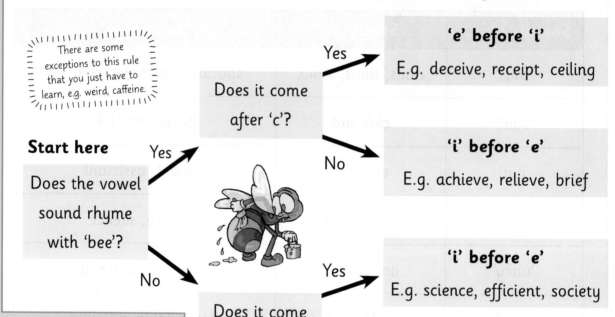

There are some exceptions to this rule that you just have to learn, e.g. weird, caffeine.

Start here

Does the vowel sound rhyme with 'bee'?

Yes → Does it come after 'c'?

Yes → **'e' before 'i'** E.g. deceive, receipt, ceiling

No → **'i' before 'e'** E.g. achieve, relieve, brief

No → Does it come after 'c'?

Yes → **'i' before 'e'** E.g. science, efficient, society

No → **Could be either** E.g. height, fried, weight

Homophones

Homophones: words that sound the same, but have different meanings and spellings

Make sure you use the correct homophone when you're writing, e.g. '<u>They're</u> travelling <u>there</u> in <u>their</u> spaceship'.

EXAMPLE

rain: water from the sky

reign: the rule of a king or queen

rein: a strap used to guide a horse

Confusing Nouns & Verbs

Some nouns and verbs sound similar but are spelt differently.

Normally, the word with a 'c' is a noun and the word with an 's' is a verb.

Silent Letters

Silent letters: letters in a word that you don't hear

Silent 'k'
E.g. knot, knight, knee

Silent 'b'
E.g. tomb, climb, debt

Silent 'l'
E.g. would, calm, chalk

Others
E.g. sign, yacht, ghost

'ough' Words

Words that contain the letters 'ough' can sound very different.

Sound	Examples
'ow'	plough, drought
'uf'	tough, rough
'or'	sought, fought
'uh'	borough, thorough
'oh'	although, dough

Saying the two words out loud can help. E.g. the 's' in 'advise' sounds different to the 'c' in 'advice'.

Noun	Verb
device	devise
prophecy	prophesy
practice	practise

EXAMPLE

At football practice, we practised penalties.

Types of Text

Fiction & Non-Fiction

Fiction: texts about imaginary people and events

Non-fiction: texts that contain information and are based on facts

Stories

The purpose of stories is to entertain the reader.

Key features of stories:

- usually have a main character and often a villain
- have a beginning, a middle and an end

These are just a few examples. There are many other types of stories.

Types of stories

Legends

- passed down through generations
- often part made-up and part based on real events

Fantasy Stories

- set in a magical or imaginary world
- often involve a quest

Mystery Stories

- main character is often a detective solving a crime
- often a twist (an unexpected ending)

Other Types of Fiction

Poems

- usually split into verses
- often read aloud
- use techniques like rhyme and repetition

Plays

- performed on stage
- include dialogue (characters talking)
- give stage directions so actors know what to do

Audience, Purpose & Themes

Audience: who a text is for

Purpose: the reason a text has been written

Themes: the key ideas or messages in a text

Types of Non-Fiction

Most non-fiction texts fit into one or more of these categories.

Non-chronological means 'not in time order'.

Type of text	Purpose
Report	gives information on a topic, often in non-chronological order
Persuasive text	persuades people to think or do something
Explanation text	explains how a process works
Instruction text	tells people how to do something
Discussion text	shares arguments for and against a topic
Recount	retells an event or series of events

EXAMPLE

① A recipe for biscuits ⟹ Instruction text

② An advert for a new zoo ⟹ Persuasive text

③ An autobiography by a famous guitarist ⟹ Recount

Reading Skills

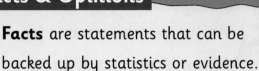

Working Out Meanings

If you're not sure what a word or phrase means:

1 Find clues in the text — look for other words you do understand.

2 See if it's part of a word family — use this to guess the meaning.

3 Look it up in a dictionary.

Facts & Opinions

Facts are statements that can be backed up by statistics or evidence.

Volcanoes can be found on land and on the ocean floor.

This information can be proven with evidence.

Finding Information

Sometimes, information is stated clearly in a text. This is called fact retrieval.

EXAMPLE

River otters give birth between February and April and have up to five babies per year.

The text says that otters can have up to five babies every year.

Sometimes, you have to use clues in the text to work it out. This is called inference.

Support your answers with quotes from the text. Always put them in inverted commas.

EXAMPLE

Suddenly, the door swung shut and Tao jumped. His entire body was trembling.

The text tells you that Tao "jumped" and his body was "trembling". These clues suggest he feels scared.

Opinions are personal views.

I think pigs are amazing.

opinion word

That pig is the best pig in the world.

Opinions often use exaggerated language.

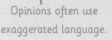

Analysing Texts

You could be asked to:

1 **summarise** a text by explaining its main message or ideas.

EXAMPLE

Paragraph 1: Rugby is good exercise.

Paragraph 2: It teaches teamwork.

Paragraph 3: It helps to reduce stress.

Summary: Rugby is good for you.

2 **make a comparison** between texts or parts of a text.

Things you could compare:

- the key themes
- the mood of the text
- the characters' goals, how they feel or their relationships

3 **predict** what will happen next.

- What has happened so far?
- How are the characters feeling?
- Are there clues about what's next?

Structure & Language

Structure

What order are events described in?

Are there any points where things change?

How are ideas grouped together?

Language

What effect do words have?

With nerves of steel, Jen climbed daringly up the perilous cliff.

These words make Jen sound brave.

See p.18-19 for more on language.

Writing Fiction

Planning

Always plan before you start writing. Think about:

What?	plot
Where?	setting
Who?	characters

Plot

Basic story structure:

> Beginning — the scene is set

> Middle — a problem or conflict

> End — the problem has been fixed

Setting

Use descriptive language to set the scene:

adjective

verb

adverb

> The immense building loomed over us menacingly.

Starting a Story

Two great ways to begin:

1. in the middle of the action

> The wind whistled past Nick's ears as he clung to the plane's wing.

2. with a character speaking

> "Where do you think you're going?" Mrs Pike demanded.

Use speech to show a character's personality. Mrs Pike's speech makes her seem angry.

Characters

Show their appearance and personality:

> Her wrinkled face lit up with a bright smile.

appearance: old, wrinkled

personality: happy, friendly

Story Writing Checklist

Does your story have:

1 interesting characters & setting? ✓

2 a problem to be fixed? ✓

Synonyms & Antonyms

Use a thesaurus to find alternatives to common words.

Instead of...	you could say...
said	whispered, yelled, sighed, roared
big	massive, gigantic, colossal, huge

Synonyms: words with similar meanings

Antonyms: words with opposite meanings

Language Techniques

metaphor: when you say something <u>is</u> something else

simile: when you say something is <u>like</u> something else

The moon was a gleaming jewel in the sky as the terrified man crashed through the forest like a steam train.

onomatopoeia: when a word sounds like what it describes

Checking Your Writing

Always check for errors, and correct mistakes neatly.

They waved ~~there~~ their hands.

Common mistakes:

3. an effective start and ending? ✓

4. descriptive language? ✓

5. correct spelling & grammar? ✓

✗ verb not matching the subject

✗ not staying in the same tense

✗ forgetting to use paragraphs

Writing Non-Fiction

Standard English

Always use Standard English in your writing.

> Never use the negative 'ain't' in your writing — it's non-Standard English.

❌ I haven't got no time. ✅ I haven't got any time.

❌ Priya and me play tennis. ✅ Priya and I play tennis.

❌ He loves them flowers. ✅ He loves those flowers.

❌ We should of known. ✅ We should have known.

Informal & Formal Writing

Informal Writing	Formal Writing
uses chatty language e.g. I had an awesome time.	uses formal language e.g. We regret to inform you...
can use contracted forms e.g. They weren't successful.	avoids contracted forms e.g. They were not successful.
can use exclamation marks e.g. I bought a new laptop!	avoids exclamation marks e.g. I bought a new laptop.

Some formal writing uses
the subjunctive form.

It's crucial that she is on time.
It's crucial that she be on time.

If I was king, I would pass a law.
If I were king, I would pass a law.

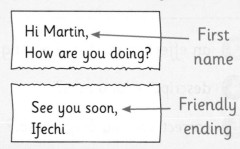

Informal letters are friendlier:

Hi Martin, ← First name
How are you doing?

See you soon, ← Friendly ending
Ifechi

20   Reading & Writing

Writing Information Texts

Layout devices make your writing clearer and more appealing.

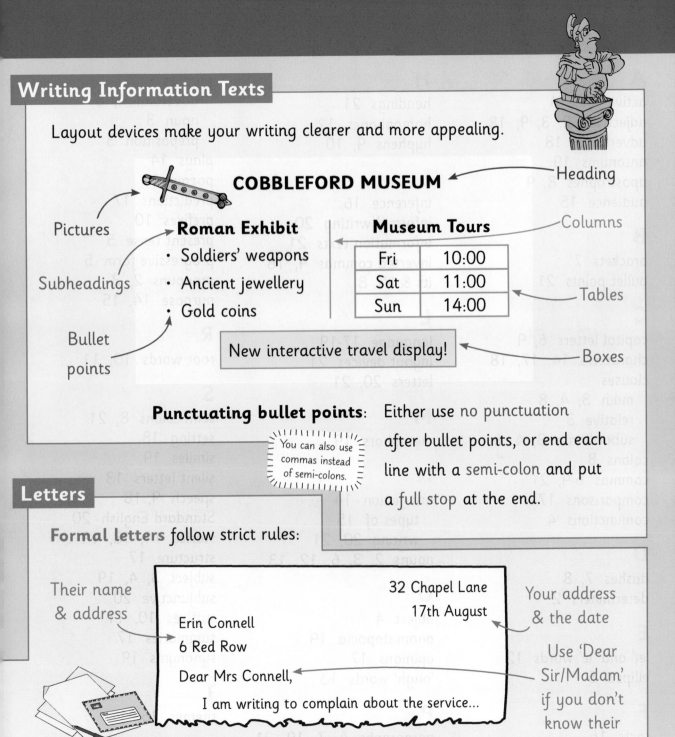

Pictures

Subheadings

Bullet points

COBBLEFORD MUSEUM ← Heading

Roman Exhibit
- Soldiers' weapons
- Ancient jewellery
- Gold coins

Museum Tours ← Columns

Fri	10:00
Sat	11:00
Sun	14:00

← Tables

New interactive travel display! ← Boxes

Punctuating bullet points: Either use no punctuation after bullet points, or end each line with a semi-colon and put a full stop at the end.

> You can also use commas instead of semi-colons.

Letters

Formal letters follow strict rules:

Their name & address

32 Chapel Lane
17th August → Your address & the date

Erin Connell
6 Red Row
Dear Mrs Connell, ← Use 'Dear Sir/Madam' if you don't know their name.

I am writing to complain about the service...

Your title & surname

Yours sincerely, ← Use 'Yours faithfully' if you
Mr Evans used 'Dear Sir/Madam'.

> Make sure you use paragraphs in both formal and informal letters.

Index